Ten in the Bed

for Felice
J.C.

Text and Illustrations © Jane Cabrera 2006
First published in Great Britain in 2006 by
Gullane Children's Books,
an imprint of Pinwheel Limited.
Winchester House, 259-269 Old Marylebone Road, London NW1 5XJ
First published in the United States of America by Holiday House, Inc. in 2006
All Rights Reserved
Manufactured in China
www.holidayhouse.com
First Edition
1 3 5 7 9 10 8 6 4 2

Library of Congress Cataloging-in-Publication Data
Cabrera, Jane.
Ten in the bed / by Jane Cabrera.— 1st ed.
p. cm.
Summary: In this version of the traditional nursery rhyme, each of the sleepers who fall, leap,
bounce, or wobble out of bed when the little one says "Move over" represents a different profession.
ISBN-13: 978-0-8234-2027-8 (hardcover)
ISBN-10: 0-8234-2027-2 (hardcover)
1.Nursery rhymes. [1. Nursery rhymes. 2. Occupations—Fiction. 3. Counting. 4. Stories in rhyme.]
I. Title: Ten in the bed. II. Title.
PZ8.3.C122Al5 2006
[E]—dc22
2005035880

Ten in the Bed

Jane Cabrera

Holiday House / New York

Here is the Little One,
A tired and sleepy head.
Stretching and yawning,
He's ready for bed.

But...

10

There were **ten** in the bed
And the **L**ittle **O**ne said,
"**M**ove over, move over."

So they all rolled over
And the **Snorer**
fell out.

So they all rushed over
And the **Cook fell out.**

There were **eight** in the bed
And the **Little One** said,
"Move over, move over."

So they all bounced over
And the **Trumpeter fell out.**

7

There were **seven** in the bed
And the **Little One** said,
"**Move** over, move over."

So they all groaned over
And the **Doctor**
fell out.

There were **SIX** in the bed
And the **Little One** said,
"**Move** over, move over."

So they all leaped over
And the **Ballerina** fell out.

5

There were **five** in the bed
And the **Little One** said,
"Move over, move over."

So they all swayed over
And the **Pirate fell out.**

4

There were **four** in the bed
And the **Little One** said,
"**M**ove over, move over."

So they all bowed over
And the **Princess fell out.**

There were
three in the bed
And the **Little One** said,
"Move over, move over."

So they all wobbled over
And the **Pilot**
fell out.

3

2

There were **TWO** in the bed
And the **Little One** said,
"Move over, move over."
So the Astronaut floated over
And **she fell out.**

There was **one** in the bed
And **everyone** said,
"Move over, move over."

So the little one moved over
And he...

…fell out!

So…

Snorer

Cook

Trumpeter

Doctor

Ballerina

...they all danced about!
Then the **Little One** screamed
And he gave a big shout...

"Settle down now, settle down now!"

So they all settled down and went to sleep.
There was not a sound, there was not a peep.
Until the Little One said . . .

"Good night!"